19.95

JAN 30 2018

MAKE IT YOURSELF!
From Junk to
JEWELRY

Carol Hove

Checkerboard Library

An Imprint of Abdo Publishing
abdopublishing.com

abdopublishing.com

Published by Abdo Publishing, a division of ABDO, PO Box 398166, Minneapolis, Minnesota 55439. Copyright © 2018 by Abdo Consulting Group, Inc. International copyrights reserved in all countries. No part of this book may be reproduced in any form without written permission from the publisher. Checkerboard Library™ is a trademark and logo of Abdo Publishing.

Printed in the United States of America, North Mankato, Minnesota
062017
092017

THIS BOOK CONTAINS RECYCLED MATERIALS

Design: Sarah DeYoung, Mighty Media, Inc.
Production: Mighty Media, Inc.
Editor: Liz Salzmann
Cover Photographs: Mighty Media, Inc.
Interior Photographs: iStockphoto; Mighty Media, Inc.; Shutterstock; Thinkstock

The following manufacturers/names appearing in this book are trademarks: Aleene's® Tacky Glue®, Elmer's® Glue-All™

Publisher's Cataloging-in-Publication Data
Names: Hove, Carol, author.
Title: Make it yourself! from junk to jewelry / by Carol Hove.
Other titles: From junk to jewelry
Description: Minneapolis, MN : Abdo Publishing, 2018. | Series: Cool makerspace | Includes bibliographical references and index.
Identifiers: LCCN 2016962823 | ISBN 9781532110702 (lib. bdg.) | ISBN 9781680788556 (ebook)
Subjects: LCSH: Makerspaces--Juvenile literature. | Handicraft--Juvenile literature.
Classification: DDC 680--dc23
LC record available at http://lccn.loc.gov/2016962823

TO ADULT HELPERS

This is your chance to assist a new maker! As children learn to use makerspaces, they develop new skills, gain confidence, and make cool things. These activities are designed to help children create projects in makerspaces. Children may need more assistance for some activities than others. Be there to offer guidance when they need it. Encourage them to do as much as they can on their own. Be a cheerleader for their creativity.

Before getting started, remember to lay down ground rules for using tools and supplies and for cleaning up.

CONTENTS

What's a MAKERSPACE?

Imagine an area buzzing with people making amazing creations. Wide-open spaces invite you to draw, design, plan, and build. And every material you could imagine is within reach!

This is a makerspace. It is a place where people come together to create all kinds of cool stuff. Makers share sparks of creativity. They love to learn something new. They work together to turn old junk and other materials into bracelets, necklaces, earrings, and more! Are you ready to become a maker?

FUN WITH JUNK TO JEWELRY

Materials are very important in a makerspace. Sometimes, specific items are needed. Other times, mystery materials inspire perfect project ideas. A space stocked with junk can lead to amazing jewelry-making **sessions**.

Discover what designs might be hiding within **discarded** odds and ends. See if you can transform them into sparkling earrings, wild wrist **bling**, and other decorative pieces.

JUNK TO JEWELRY TIPS

Sharing is an important aspect of a makerspace. Makers share workspace, materials, and ideas. Being surrounded by other makers is great for creativity. But it also means a lot of projects may be happening at once. Here are some tips for successful makerspace projects.

HAVE A PLAN

Read through a project before beginning. Research any jewelry terms you may not know. Make sure you have everything you need for the project.

ASK FOR PERMISSION

Get **permission** from an adult to use the space, tools, and supplies.

BE RESPECTFUL

Before taking a tool or material, make sure another maker isn't using it.

KEEP YOUR SPACE CLEAN

Jewelry parts are often very tiny. Keep small parts in bowls or jars. Then they won't get scattered or lost.

EXPECT MISTAKES & BE CREATIVE!

Being a maker isn't about creating something perfect. Have fun as you work!

SUPPLIES

Here are some of the materials and tools you'll need to do the projects in this book.

beading cord

beads

cord necklace

craft glue

dominoes

earring wires

electronic resistors

flat buttons

glue-on bail mounts

jewelry clasps

jewelry spacer bars

jewelry wire

jump rings

leather-like fabric

measuring
tape

needle-nose
pliers

O-rings

paper clips

pin backs

small metal
objects

super-strong
adhesive

yarn

JEWELRY TECHNIQUES

It's helpful to hold small parts with needle-nose pliers while you assemble jewelry.

To properly open or close a jump ring, hold each side of the split with a needle-nose pliers. Twist to open and twist to close. Do not pull the sides apart.

PAPER-CLIP NECKLACE

Make a statement necklace with colorful beads and paper clips!

1. Cut two or three strands of yarn. Make them each 12 inches (30 cm) longer than you want the necklace to be. Tie the strands together 6 inches (15 cm) from one end.

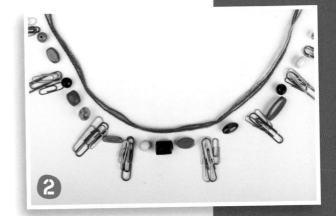

2. Lay the yarn on the table. Place paper clips and the beads along the yarn. They should go from the knot to 6 inches (15 cm) from the other end. Arrange the items the way you want your necklace to look.

3. Make a wire needle to help put the beads and clips on the yarn. Cut a piece of wire about 6 inches (15 cm) long. Bend it into a *U* shape. Put the yarn in the bend of the wire. Push the ends of the wire through the first item you want to put on the yarn. Pull the wire and yarn all the way through.

4. String the rest of the beads and clips in the order you arranged them. Tie a knot after the last item.

5. Tie a knot about ½ inch (1.3 cm) from each end of the necklace. To wear the necklace, tie the ends in a bow behind your neck.

O-RING BRACELET

Turn rubber rings into
a stylish bracelet!

WHAT YOU NEED

O-rings, different sizes

2 jump rings

needle-nose pliers

jewelry clasp

1. Lay two or more large O-rings on top of each other.

2. Place a smaller O-ring on each side of the large O-rings.

3. Wrap one of the small O-rings around the large O-rings. Push one side of the small O-ring through its center. Pull to tighten. Tie the other small O-ring to the other side of the large O-rings the same way.

4. To make the bracelet longer, add more small O-rings to each end.

5. Open a jump ring with the pliers. Put one end of the bracelet through the jump ring. Put one side of the clasp through the same jump ring. Use the pliers to close the jump ring.

6. Open the other jump ring. Use it to put the other side of the clasp on the other end of the bracelet.

 **TIP** Try this project with hair elastics instead of O-rings.

ROCK PENDANT

Decorate a rock to make
a necklace from nature!

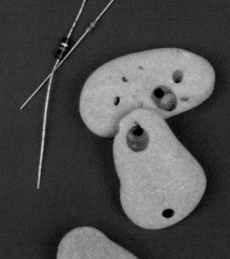

WHAT YOU NEED

rocks

electronic resistors

leather-like fabric

scissors

craft glue

cord necklace

1. Some rocks naturally have holes. These would work great for this project. You can also have an adult drill holes in your rocks.

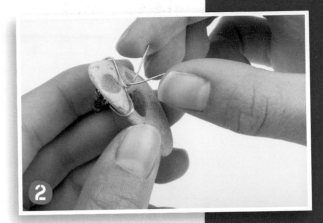

2. Lay a **resistor** on a rock. Hold it in place while wrapping the wires to the back of the rock. Twist the ends of the wires together. Add more resistors the same way.

3. Cut a piece of leather-like fabric about the size of the rock. Cut a hole in the leather to match the hole in the rock. Glue the leather to the rock over the twisted wires. Let the glue dry.

4. Fold the necklace cord in half. Put the fold through the hole in the rock. Put the ends of the cord through the loop in the cord. Pull to tighten.

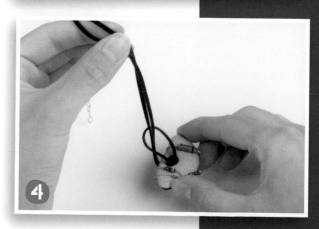

5. Try tying knots in the cord to make it look more interesting.

HARDWARE PIN

Show off your style with a unique backpack pin!

WHAT YOU NEED

card stock

marker

scissors

leather-like fabric

small metal objects, such as keys, buttons, washers, gears

craft glue

pin back

1. Decide what shape and size you want the pin to be. Draw the shape on card stock. Cut it out.

2. Trace the shape twice on the leather-like fabric. Cut out the shapes.

3. Trim the card stock shape so it's slightly smaller than the fabric pieces. Glue the fabric pieces together with the card stock between them.

4. Arrange metal objects on the pin. Try different designs until it's the way you want it. Glue the objects in place. Let the glue dry.

5. Glue the pin back to the back of the pin. Let the glue dry.

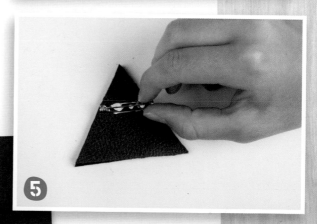

 TIP For heavy objects, you may need to use a super-strong adhesive.

LOCK & KEY BRACELET

Use small locks and keys to make a charming charm bracelet!

WHAT YOU NEED

measuring tape

metal chain

needle-nose pliers

jewelry clasp

small metal locks & keys

jump rings

1. Measure around your wrist. If necessary, shorten the chain to match the measurement. Use the pliers to open and remove links from the chain.

2. Open the link at one end of the chain. Put one side of the clasp on the link and close it. Put the other side of the clasp on the other end the same way.

3. Lay the chain on the table. Place the locks and keys along the chain. Arrange them the way you want your bracelet to look.

4. Attach each object to the chain with a jump ring.

TIP Make sure the chain is sturdy enough to hold the weight of the objects. And the links need to be big enough for the jump rings to fit through them.

BUTTON EARRINGS

Make dangling earrings to go with any outfit!

1. Choose three or four buttons. Decide which will be the top button. The other buttons will hang from it.

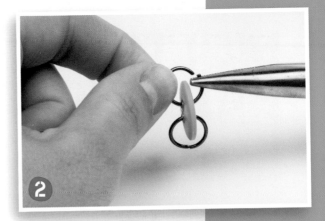

2. Attach two jump rings to the top button. Place them opposite each other.

3. Attach a jump ring to one of the rings on the top button. This is the mid ring.

4. Use jump rings to attach the other buttons to the mid ring.

5. Attach an earring wire to the other ring on the top button.

6. Repeat steps 1 through 5 to make the second earring.

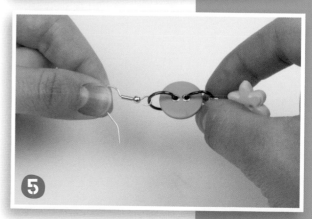

MULTI-STRAND BEAD BRACELET

Wrap wires around beads to create
a beaded bracelet!

1. Cut five or more strands of jewelry wire. Make them each 24 inches (61 cm) long.

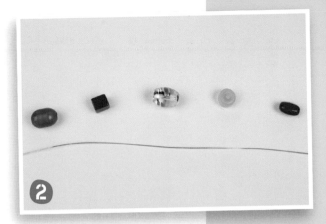

2. Lay a strand of wire on the table. Place beads along the wire. Arrange the beads the way you want your bracelet to look.

3. Thread the first bead on the wire. Pull all but 5 inches (13 cm) of the wire through the bead. Hold the bead in place. Thread the long end of the wire through the bead again. Pull the wire tight to keep the bead in place.

4. Thread the next bead on the long end of the wire. Leave as much space as you want between it and the first bead. Hold the bead in place and thread the wire through the bead again. Pull the wire tight.

5. Repeat step 4 to add the rest of the beads. Leave 5 inches (13 cm) at the end of the wire empty.

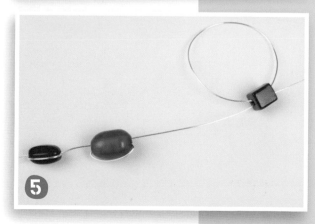

Continued on the next page.

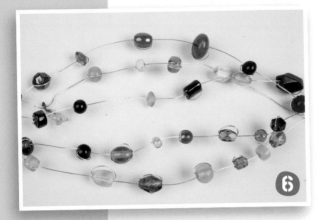

6 Repeat steps 2 through 5 to put beads on the other strands of wire.

7. Lay the beaded wires next to one another. Twist the wires together at one end. Then twist the wires together at the other end.

8. Trim the ends so the wires are even. But leave several inches of twisted wire at each end of the bracelet.

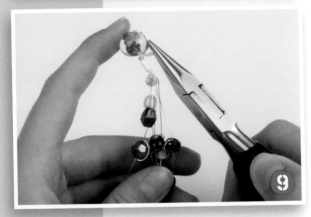

9 Thread one end of the bracelet though a large bead. Bring the end back over the bead. Twist the end around the wire to keep the bead in place. This bead will be one half of the clasp.

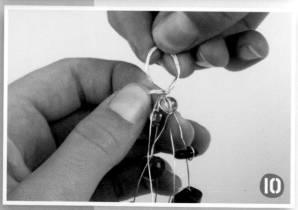

10 Bend the other end of the bracelet into a loop. Twist the end around the wire. The loop should be slightly larger than the bead you added in step 9. The loop is the other half of the clasp.

11. Wrap the bracelet around your wrist. Push the large bead through the loop to secure the bracelet.

BRIGHT IDEA!

You can find beads and other jewelry supplies in craft stores and **thrift stores**. Or ask at home for jewelry you can take apart and reuse. Sort your supplies by color, size, and material. Keep them in clear containers. When choosing items for a project, dump a container into a bowl. Use a spoon to pick up a few items at a time to look at!

DOMINO JEWELRY SET

Turn dominoes into a
necklace, a bracelet,
and earrings!

Necklace

1. Cut a piece of beading cord a little longer than you want the necklace to be.

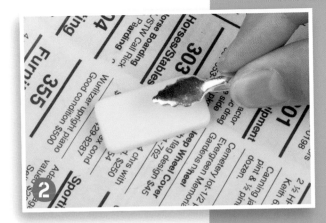

2. Choose the dominoes you want to use on the necklace. Cover your work surface with newspaper. Glue a bail mount to the back of each chosen domino. Let the glue dry.

3. Use the dominoes and some beads to create an arrangement for the necklace. Thread the dominoes and beads on the cord.

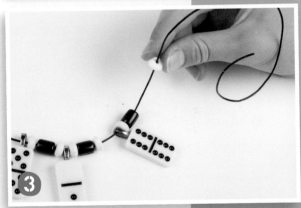

4. Tie one side of the clasp to each end of the necklace.

Continued on the next page.

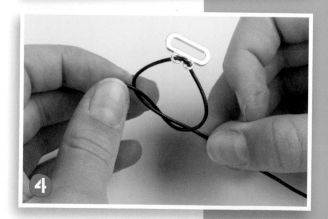

Bracelet

1. Measure around your wrist. If necessary, shorten the chain to match the measurement. Use the pliers to open and remove links from the chain.

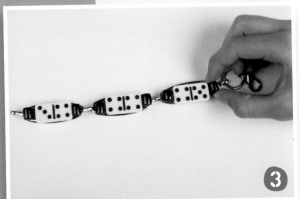

2. Use pliers to attach one side of the clasp to each end of the chain.

3. Lay dominoes and beads on the chain to create a design.

4. Cover your work surface with newspaper. Glue the dominoes and beads to the chain. Let the glue dry.

Earrings

1. Use the pliers to attach an earring wire to an end hole in each spacer bar.

2. Choose a domino for each earring.

3. Cover your work surface with newspaper. Glue a space bar to the back of each domino. Let the glue dry.

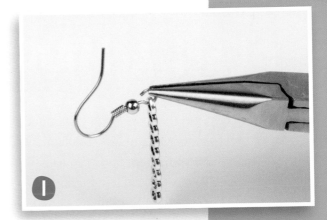

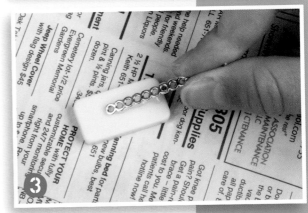

TIP The pieces in this project were made with small dominoes. But larger dominoes can also work great depending upon your design.

PLAN A MAKER EVENT!

Being a maker is not just about the finished product. It is about communication, **collaboration**, and creativity. Do you have a project you'd like to make with the support of a group? Then make a plan and set it in action!

SECURE A SPACE

Think of places that would work well for a makerspace. This could be a library, school classroom, or space in a community center. Then, talk to adults in charge of the space. Describe your project. Tell them how you would use the space and keep it organized and clean.

INVITE MAKERS

Once you have a space, it is time to spread the word! Work with adults in charge of the space to determine how to do this. You could make an e-invitation, create flyers about your maker event, or have family and friends tell others.

MATERIALS & TOOLS

Materials and tools cost money. How will you supply these things? **Brainstorm** ways to raise money for your makerspace. You could plan a fund-raiser to buy needed items. You could also ask makers to bring their own supplies.

GLOSSARY

bling — flashy jewelry.

brainstorm — to come up with a solution by having all members of a group share ideas.

collaboration — the act of working with another person or group in order to do something or reach a goal.

discard — to throw away.

permission — when a person in charge says it's okay to do something.

resistor — a device that is used to control the flow of electricity in an electric circuit.

session — a period of time used for a specific purpose or activity.

thrift store — a store that sells used items, especially one that is run by a charity.

WEBSITES

To learn more about Cool Makerspace, visit **abdobooklinks.com**. These links are routinely monitored and updated to provide the most current information available.

INDEX